Dear Parents,

This coloring book is designed for young children who love L.O.L Surprise! Help your little ones celebrate their love of L.O.L. Surprise Dolls with this big full-page coloring book that is perfect for little hands. This book will provide hours of coloring fun and the easy to color designs will help to build fine-motor skills and hand-eye coordination.

What makes this coloring book different from others:

1. Big simple pictures perfect for beginners
2. Drawings designed so it's easy to stay inside the lines
3. Thick outlines and large areas to color
4. No movie or cartoon characters
5. Large 8 1/2 x 11 inch pages

Coloring is fun for kids and has lots of benefits including:

1. Improves fine motor skills
2. Prepares children for school
3. Contributes to better handwriting
4. Color awareness and recognition
5. Improves focus and hand eye coordination
6. Makes a great gift!

Cute L.O.L Surprise Coloring Book for Boys and Girls!

We would love to hear from you. If you have any feedback, please email us at eparker125@yahoo.com

check
meow-out

a big
Heart
of an
Angel

Splash into
a new
LOL!

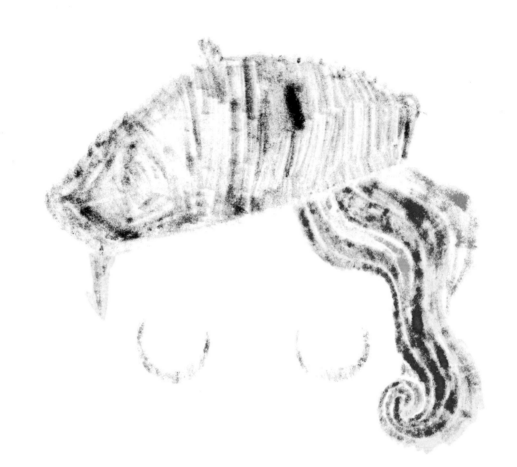

You're The Best!

Thank you again for getting this coloring book!

I hope this book was able to help **celebrate the joy of L.O.L Surprise Dolls!**

The next step is to share your colored pictures.

Finally, if you enjoyed this book, then I'd like to ask you for a favor, would you be kind enough to leave a review for this book on Amazon? It'd be greatly appreciated!

Leave a review for this book on Amazon today!

Check Out These Other Books

Below you'll find some other popular L.O.L. Surprise Books that are popular on Amazon as well. Simply search them out... Alternatively, you can email me at eparker125@yahoo.com or visit my author page to see other work done by me at amazon.com/author/evelynparker

L.O.L. Surprise Lil Sisters!

L.O.L. Surprise Pets!

L.O.L. Surprise! Picture Book – Series 1

AND MUCH MORE!!!

You can simply search for these titles on the Amazon website to find them.

Made in the USA
Middletown, DE
29 July 2018